Banana Bread Recipes

Every Kind of Banana Bread You Could Think of and Beyond!

BY

Brian White

Copyright 2021 Brian White

Copyright Page

This book is under license, which means you are not allowed to copy, print, publish distribute or disseminate the content inside. The only person who can do these changes is the author. Also, this book is for informational purposes. The author made sure that everything in this book is accurate but you still need to take every step and decision with caution.

In case you end up getting a copied and illegal version of this e-book please report it and delete the book and get the original version. In this way, you will support the author and he will be able to make more fantastic books like this one.

Table of Contents

Introduction 6

Chapter 1: Fun Facts About Bananas and Banana Bread 8

Chapter 2: Recipes 10

    Recipe 1: Almond Banana Bread 11

    Recipe 2: Almost No Fat Banana Bread 14

    Recipe 3: Apple and Walnut Banana Bread 16

    Recipe 4: Apricot Banana Bread 19

    Recipe 5: Apricot-Banana Quick Bread 21

    Recipe 6: Banana Almond Bread 23

    Recipe 7: Banana and Ginger Cupcakes 25

    Recipe 8: Banana Muffins 27

    Recipe 9: Banana Apple Bread 29

    Recipe 10: Ever banana Bread 32

    Recipe 11: Banana-Berry Nut Bread 34

    Recipe 12: Banana Blueberry Bread 36

    Recipe 13: Banana-Blueberry Buttermilk Bread 38

    Recipe 14: Banana Bran Muffins 41

    Recipe 15: Banana Bran Zucchini Bread 43

    Recipe 16: Anytime Banana Bread 46

    Recipe 17: Oatmeal Bars 48

Recipe 18: Bread Cookies 50

Recipe 19: Banana Bread Brownies... 52

Recipe 20: Banana Chocolate Pudding 55

Recipe 21: Banana Bread Cobbler.. 57

Recipe 22: Banana Bread Cookies.. 59

Recipe 23: Donuts with Browned Butter Caramel Glaze 61

Recipe 24: Banana Bread French Toast 64

Recipe 25: Banana Bread from Motts 66

Recipe 26: Banana Bread Muffins.. 68

Recipe 27: Banana Cream Cheese Glaze 70

Recipe 28: Bread Protein Waffles 73

Recipe 29: Banana Bread Pudding 75

Recipe 30: Banana Streusel Muffins... 78

Recipe 31: Banana Chia Seeds.. 80

Recipe 32: Banana Bread with Chocolate Filling... 82

Recipe 33: Banana Bread with Cream Cheese 85

Recipe 34: Banana Bread with Maple Flavor 87

Recipe 35: Banana Bread with Mayonnaise 89

Recipe 36: Banana Bread with Oat-Streusel Topping 91

Recipe 37: Banana Bread with Salted Caramel.. 94

Recipe 38: Banana Bread with Vanilla Pudding 96

Recipe 39: Banana Bread with Walnuts 99

Recipe 40: Banana Butterscotch Bread 101

Recipe 41: Banana Chai Bread 103

Recipe 42: Banana Chip Bread 105

Recipe 43: Banana-Chip Nut Bread 107

Recipe 44: Banana Chocolate Chip Bread 109

Recipe 45: Banana Chocolate Chip Muffins 111

Recipe 46: Banana Flaxseed Muffins 113

Recipe 47: Banana Coconut Loaf 115

Recipe 48: Banana Cranberry Bread 117

Recipe 49: Banana Date Flaxseed Bread 119

Recipe 50: Banana Eggnog Bread 121

Conclusion 123

Afterthoughts 124

About the Author 125

Introduction

Healthy banana bread

Get excited because you are about to try some new banana bread unlike any you have ever had before. Just when you thought banana bread was basic and getting a little boring, you have to think again because it is anything but boring! There are so many ways to make new and exciting banana bread that it was hard to fit all the ideas into one cookbook. However, we managed to sort through all the new banana bread ideas and create these perfect ones. They are easy to follow, quick to make, and give you some of the best banana bread you have ever tried. I made this banana bread cookbook because, well, I'm just obsessed with banana bread. After making the same old loaf time and time again, I knew it was time for something different.

While I love my regular banana bread (and you will too, which is why I included that recipe!), it was time to spice it up. I started experimenting with what tastes good inside banana bread and switching a few ingredients here and there until I found what works best. Now, I pass them to you! Amazing banana bread recipes that keep the essence of the original banana bread but are still much more adventurous than having just bananas baked in.

Baked banana bread has no equal. The aroma reminds me of snack time after school when my mother would give us a slice of fresh banana bread with a glass of milk. The texture and taste of the sweet bread were delightful, and we stuffed our faces with glee! My kids enjoyed this kind of snack as much as I did, so I attempted to vary the recipe every time. The following 300+ recipes are some of my favorite banana nut bread methods that have hit my family. Try one today and start your special traditions with this delicious and healthy snack.

Whether you are a novice baker or a professional, you will love these recipes, and there is something new for everyone. Give the coconut chocolate chip a try when you need something rich and tropical, and then bake the apple walnut loaf for a more warm and dense treat. No matter what you make first, you will be impressed with your baking skills and obsessed with your newfound love for interesting banana bread. Grab those overripe bananas and get ready to bake!

Chapter 1: Fun Facts About Bananas and Banana Bread

We all love banana bread!

It's one of the most basic sweet snacks globally, but it's also one of the most delectable. I'm sure you've heard that overripe bananas are ideal for banana bread, but did you realize that banana bread isn't bread? Or that it is very beneficial to your heart? Continue reading to learn more fascinating facts about your favorite treat.

In the 1930s, rising agents such as baking powder and baking soda were invented, and banana bread became quite popular. Previously, pearlash was utilized by housewives.

Banana bread is excellent for your heart, and bananas are solely responsible. The potassium content helps control blood pressure and heart function. Bananas also have a low glycemic index, providing an energy boost. This makes banana bread a great breakfast treat!

Bananas came to the US in the 1870s and were quickly used as sweets. Bananas are currently the most popular fruit in America, with 90% of households buying them monthly. We're guessing that a lot of them wind up in banana bread recipes.

Finally, every single one of your banana bread recipes is a mutant! The familiar yellow banana that we all eat and enjoy is a genetic variant of several different banana types (more than 500, more precisely). It's also the sweetest of the bunch. Bananas can come in various hues, including those that are bright pink and taste like strawberries. They also come in various sizes and forms, ranging from enormous purple plantains to little finger fruits.

So, what do you have to lose? Find some pink bananas in the wild. It's time to spice up banana bread recipes!

Chapter 2: Recipes

Recipe 1: Almond Banana Bread

This banana bread has nice crunchy almonds added to it, but it also has flavorful almond flour. Using almond flour makes the bread dense and moist, exactly what you want in banana bread!

Serving Size: 4

Cooking Time: 10 minutes

Ingredients:

- ½ cup butter softened
- 1 cup dark brown sugar
- 2 eggs, whisked
- 1 tsp almond extract
- 1/8 tsp kosher salt
- 1 cup flour
- 1 cup almond flour
- 1 ½ tsp baking soda
- 3 large ripe bananas
- ½ cup chopped almond

Directions:

Blend the butter and dark brown sugar in a stand mixer equipped with the paddle attachment until frothy and light. Scrape down the basin a few times to incorporate all the sugar and butter.

Add the ripe bananas to the bowl and mix as well. The mixer will mash the bananas nicely with the sugar, so there is no need to mash them beforehand! If you are making the banana bread by hand and do not have a stand mixer, then be sure to mash the bananas well and incorporate them fully into the sugar mix- there should be no lumps!

Add the eggs and almond extract to the bowl and blend well. The batter may look a little separated, but that is okay; it will come together soon!

In a mixing bowl, combine all dry ingredients. Scrape the edges of the basin to make sure everything is thoroughly combined. The batter will be thick and smooth.

Fold the chopped almonds into the batter, mixing until they are fully distributed.

Pour the batter into a prepared loaf pan and bake for an hour at 350°F. It will gently peel away from the pan's sides, and a knife put into the middle will come out clean.

After 15 minutes, turn the bread out onto a wire cooling rack.

Recipe 2: Almost No Fat Banana Bread

Yummy banana bread

Serving Size: 4

Cooking Time: 55 minutes

Ingredients:

- 3/4 cup white sugar
- 1 1/4 tsp baking powder
- 1/2 tsp ground cinnamon
- 2 egg whites
- 1 cup banana, mashed
- 1/2 tsp baking soda
- 1/4 cup applesauce
- 1 1/2 cups all-purpose flour

Directions:

Preheat the oven to 175 °C or 350 °F. Grease a loaf pan of 8x4 inches in size lightly.

Mix sugar, baking soda, flour, baking powder, and cinnamon in a big bowl. Put in applesauce, bananas, and egg whites; mix just till blended. Put batter into prepped pan.

Bake for 50-55 minutes, or until a toothpick inserted into the bread comes out clean. Transfer to wire rack and let cool before slicing.

Recipe 3: Apple and Walnut Banana Bread

Apples and walnuts are an amazing combination, and then, when added to banana bread, magic happens. This banana bread loaf is rich and moist with a slight crunch (thanks to the walnuts) and pieces of flavor-packed right (thanks to the apple). A perfect fall recipe to try!

Serving Size: 4

Cooking Time: 10 minutes

Ingredients:

- ½ cup butter softened
- 1 cup dark brown sugar
- 2 eggs, whisked
- 1 ¼ tsp baking soda
- 1 tsp vanilla extract
- 1/8 tsp kosher salt
- 2 cups flour
- 3 large ripe bananas
- 1 cup chopped walnuts
- 1 cup diced apple

Directions:

In a stand mixer, beat butter and dark brown sugar until light and frothy. Scrape down the basin a few times to incorporate all the sugar and butter.

Add the ripe bananas to the bowl and mix as well. The mixer will mash the bananas nicely with the sugar, so there is no need to mash them beforehand! If you are making the banana bread by hand and do not have a stand mixer, then be sure to mash the bananas well and incorporate them fully into the sugar mix- there should be no lumps!

Mix in the eggs and vanilla essence. The batter may seem divided now, but it will come together shortly!

In a mixing bowl, combine all dry ingredients. Scrape the edges of the basin to make sure everything is thoroughly combined. The batter will be thick and smooth.

Fold the walnuts and diced apples into the batter, mixing until they are fully distributed.

Pour the batter into a prepared loaf pan and bake for an hour at 350°F. It will gently peel away from the pan's sides, and a knife put into the middle will come out clean.

After 15 minutes, turn the bread out onto a wire cooling rack. Keep at room temperature for a week or two.

Recipe 4: Apricot Banana Bread

A delicious twist for banana bread

Serving Size: 16

Cooking Time: 1 hour and 10 minutes

Ingredients:

- 1 tsp baking powder
- 2 eggs
- 1 cup of mashed ripe bananas
- 2/3 cup sugar
- 1/4 cup buttermilk
- 1-1/4 cups all-purpose flour
- 1/2 tsp salt
- 1/3 cup butter
- 1 cup 100% bran cereal (not flakes)
- 1/2 tsp baking soda
- 3/4 cup chopped dried apricots (about 6-ounce)
- 1/2 cup chopped walnuts

Directions:

In a large bowl, cream sugar and butter; mix in eggs. Bananas and buttermilk Alternately add salt, baking soda, baking powder, and flour to creamed mixture, mixing thoroughly after each addition. Mix nuts, apricots, and bran in.

Put in 9x5-in. Greased loaf pan; bake for 55-60 minutes at 350° till an inserted toothpick in the middle exits clean. Cool for 10 minutes before transferring to the wire rack.

Recipe 5: Apricot-Banana Quick Bread

Yummy bread

Serving Size: 16

Cooking Time: 1 hour and 20 minutes

Ingredients:

- 1/4 cup butter, softened
- 3/4 cup sugar
- 2 large eggs
- 1 cup mashed ripe bananas
- 1-2/3 cups all-purpose flour
- 2/3 cup toasted wheat germ
- 2 tsp baking powder
- 1/4 tsp salt
- 1/4 tsp baking soda
- 1 cup finely chopped dried apricots
- 2 tsp grated lemon peel

Directions:

Beat sugar and butter for 2 minutes until crumbly in a large bowl. One by one, add eggs, beating thoroughly after every addition; beat bananas in. Mix salt, baking soda, baking powder, wheat germ, and flour; slowly beat into the banana mixture. Mix lemon peel and apricots in.

Put in 9x5-in. Loaf pan that's coated in cooking spray.

Bake for 60-70 minutes at 350° till an inserted toothpick in the middle exits cleanly; cool for 10 minutes. Remove from pan; put on wire rack.

Recipe 6: Banana Almond Bread

Nutritious bread

Serving Size: 4

Cooking Time: 1 hour

Ingredients:

- 1 tsp vanilla extract
- 2 cups mashed ripe banana
- 1/2 cup vegetable oil
- 3 eggs
- 2 cups all-purpose flour
- 1 tsp baking soda
- 1/2 cup light brown sugar
- 1/2 tsp baking powder
- 1/2 tsp salt
- 1 1/2 cups chopped almonds
- 1/2 cup granulated sugar

Directions:

Preheat the oven to 350°. Spray a 9" x 5" loaf pan with nonstick cooking spray. Add the banana, granulated sugar, brown sugar, vegetable oil, eggs, and vanilla extract to a mixing bowl. Whisk until the batter is well combined.

Combine the baking powder, salt, baking soda, all-purpose flour, and almonds in a large mixing bowl. Only stir the batter until it is wet and blended. Pour the batter into the pan that has been prepared.

Bake the bread for 50 minutes, or until a toothpick inserted in the middle comes out clean. Take the bread out of the oven. Allow 10 minutes for the bread to cool in the pan. Before slicing, remove the bread from the pan and allow it to cool fully.

Recipe 7: Banana and Ginger Cupcakes

Banana and gingerbread spice come together to deliver warm spiced, fluffy cupcakes that the whole family can enjoy.

Serving Size: 12

Cooking Time: 25 minutes

Ingredients:

- ½ cup butter
- 3½ ounces stevia powder
- 1 cup banana flour
- 2 eggs
- 3 tbsp milk
- ¼ tsp vanilla extract
- ¼ tsp gingerbread spice
- 1 ripe banana (peeled and mashed)

Directions:

Preheat the main oven to 375 degrees F. Using cases line a 12-cup muffin tin.

First, melt the butter.

Combine the melted butter with stevia, banana flour, eggs, milk, vanilla, gingerbread spice, and mashed banana in a bowl. Stir until just combined.

Bake it in the preheated oven for 18-20 minutes, or until springy to the touch.

Recipe 8: Banana Muffins

Tasty and yummy muffins

Serving Size: 6

Cooking Time: 40 minutes

Ingredients:

- 1 1/2 tsp ground cinnamon
- 1 egg
- 1/2 tsp salt
- 3/4 cup white sugar
- 2 tsp vanilla extract
- 1 Hachiya persimmon
- 1 1/2 cups all-purpose flour
- 1/3 cup coconut oil
- 1 1/2 tsp baking powder
- 2 ripe bananas
- 1 tbsp white sugar

Directions:

Set oven to preheat at 375°F (190°C). Place paper liners on six muffin cups.

Mash persimmon and bananas together in the mixing bowl of a stand mixer. Stir in egg, 3/4 cup sugar, vanilla extract, and coconut oil, one at a time. Mix well after each addition.

Sift flour, salt, and baking powder in another bowl. Add to the fruit mixture with a spoon, just until mixed with the batter. Pour batter up to 3/4 of the muffin cups.

Stir cinnamon and 1 tbsp Sugar in a bowl. Add and sprinkle over the batter.

Serve and enjoy after 25 minutes.

Recipe 9: Banana Apple Bread

A fall-inspired banana bread recipe.

Serving Size: 30

Cooking Time: 1 hour and 25 minutes

Ingredients:

- 1 cup plain Greek yogurt
- 1/2 tsp salt
- 3 large, very ripe bananas
- 1 cup butter
- 1 tsp baking soda
- 2 cups white sugar
- 4 eggs
- 2 apples
- 1 1/2 tsp vanilla extract
- 2 3/4 cups all-purpose flour
- 3/4 cup chopped walnuts (optional)
- 1/2 cup packed brown sugar
- 1/2 cup white sugar
- 1 tbsp ground cinnamon
- 3 tbsp butter softened
- 2 tsp ground cinnamon
- banana slices for garnish
- apple slices for garnish

Directions:

Whisk salt, baking soda, 2 tsp Cinnamon and 2 3/4 cups flour till combined thoroughly in a bowl. Beat 2 cups sugar and melted butter till smooth in another mixing bowl; one by one, mix eggs in then vanilla extract and Greek yogurt. Mix flour mixture in till just incorporated.

Fold chopped walnuts, apples, and bananas in till combined; don't overmix. Small banana chunks should be visible in the batter. Put 1/2 batter in each prepped loaf pan.

Mic 3 tbsp Softened butter, 1/4 cup flour, 1 tbsp Cinnamon, 1/2 cup white sugar, and brown sugar till it looks like coarse crumbs in the bowl. Sprinkle 1/2 crumb topping on each loaf; use apple slices and bananas to garnish each loaf.

In a preheated oven, bake for 30 minutes; remove. Use aluminum foil to cover each pan. Put in the oven; bake till an inserted toothpick in the middle of loaves exits clean for 15-20 minutes. Cool, then serve.

Recipe 10: Ever banana Bread

Appetizing meal

Serving Size: 4

Cooking Time: 45 minutes

Ingredients:

- 2 1/3 cups mashed overripe bananas
- 2 eggs, beaten
- 2 cups all-purpose flour
- 1 tsp baking soda
- 1/2 cup butter
- 3/4 cup brown sugar
- 1/4 tsp salt

Directions:

Preheat an oven to 175°C/350°F; grease 9x5-in. Loaf pan lightly.

Mix salt, baking soda, and flour in a big bowl. Cream brown sugar and butter in another bowl; mix mashed bananas and eggs in till blended well. Put batter in a prepped loaf pan.

In a preheated oven, bake for 60-65 minutes till an inserted toothpick in the middle of the loaf exits cleanly; cool bread for 10 minutes in a pan. Turn out on wire rack.

Recipe 11: Banana-Berry Nut Bread

A wonderful mix of flavors.

Serving Size: 16

Cooking Time: 1 hour and 10 minutes

Ingredients:

- 1-1/2 cups all-purpose flour
- 1 tsp ground cinnamon
- 1/2 tsp baking soda
- 1/2 tsp salt
- 1/4 tsp ground nutmeg
- 2 eggs
- 1 cup sugar
- 1/4 cup canola oil
- 3/4 cup mashed fresh strawberries
- 1/2 cup of the mashed ripe banana (about 1 large)
- 1/2 to 1 cup chopped walnuts

Directions:

Mix the initial 5 ingredients in a big bowl. Whisk oil, sugar, and eggs till smooth in another bowl; add banana and strawberries. Mix wet ingredients into the dry mixture until barely moistened; fold in walnuts.

Bake for 60-65 minutes at 350°Cool for 10 minutes; transfer from pan onto a wire rack.

Recipe 12: Banana Blueberry Bread

Blueberry tasty bread

Serving Size: 15

Cooking Time: 15 minutes

Ingredients:

- ½ tsp of salt
- 1 cup of white sugar
- 2 eggs
- 2 cups of all-purpose flour
- 2 tsp of vanilla extract
- 2 ripe bananas
- 1 tsp of baking soda
- 1 cup of fresh blueberries
- ½ cup of butter

Directions:

Cream butter and sugar. Combine the eggs, mashed bananas, and vanilla extract in a mixing bowl.

Combine flour, baking soda, and salt. Toss in with the banana mixture.

Add the blueberries and mix well.

Spoon the batter into the loaf pan. Bake for 30-35 minutes in the oven

Remove from the oven and let cool for 10 minutes.

Recipe 13: Banana-Blueberry Buttermilk Bread

Buttermilk tenderizes and moistens baked goods added to the winning combination of bananas and blueberries, and the result is a great bread

Serving Size: 10

Cooking Time: 3 hours and 20 minutes

Ingredients:

- ¾ cup nonfat or low-fat buttermilk
- ¾ cup packed light brown sugar
- ¼ cup canola oil
- 2 large eggs
- 1 cup of mashed ripe banana
- 1¼ cups whole-wheat pastry flour
- 1 cup all-purpose flour
- 1½ tsp baking powder
- ¾ tsp ground cinnamon
- ½ tsp baking soda
- ½ tsp salt
- ¼ tsp ground nutmeg
- 1¼ cups blueberries, fresh or frozen

Directions:

Preheat the oven to 375°F. With cooking spray, coat a 9×5-inch loaf pan.

In a big bowl, mix eggs, oil, brown sugar, and buttermilk. Mix in crushed bananas.

Mix nutmeg, salt, baking soda, cinnamon, baking powder, all-purpose flour, and whole-wheat pastry flour in a medium bowl.

Fold dry ingredients into wet ingredients and mix till just incorporated. Fold in the blueberries. Put batter into prepped pan.

Allow baking for 50 minutes to an hour till the top is golden brown and a wooden skewer pricked in the middle comes out clean. After 10 minutes, turn out onto a wire rack. Let cool for 2 hours before slicing.

Muffin Variation: Preheat the oven to 400°F. Coat 12 (a 1/2 cup) muffin cups using cooking spray or line using paper liners. Distribute batter among muffin cups, and they will be full. A wooden skewer put into a muffin comes out clean after 20-25 minutes of baking. Remove from pan and cool for 5 minutes before serving.

Recipe 14: Banana Bran Muffins

You can use extra ripe bananas for this. Add some dark chocolate chips to make kids want to eat this!

Serving Size: 12

Cooking Time: 1 hour

Ingredients:

- ¾ cup all-purpose flour
- 2 large eggs
- 1 cup unprocessed wheat bran
- ½ tsp ground cinnamon
- 1 cup whole-wheat flour
- 1 cup buttermilk
- ¼ cup canola oil
- ⅔ cup packed light brown sugar
- 1 tsp vanilla extract
- ¼ tsp salt
- ½ tsp baking soda
- 1½ tsp baking powder
- 1 cup mashed ripe bananas, (2 medium)

Directions:

Mix brown sugar and eggs until smooth. Whisk in vanilla, oil, wheat bran, buttermilk, and bananas.

Whisk in salt, cinnamon, baking soda, baking powder, all-purpose flour, and whole-wheat flour in a big bowl. Create a well in the dry ingredients. Add wet ingredients. With a rubber spatula, mix just until combined. Mix in chocolate chips (optional). Scoop batter into prepped muffin cups; they'll be quite full. If using, sprinkle on walnuts.

Bake muffins for 15-25 minutes until it springs back when lightly touched and tops are golden brown. Cool for 5 minutes in the pan. Loosen edges. Turn out muffins on a wire rack. Slightly cool, then serve.

Recipe 15: Banana Bran Zucchini Bread

Nutritions bread

Serving Size: 20

Cooking Time: 3 hours and 20 minutes

Ingredients:

- 1/4 cup canned pumpkin
- 1 very ripe banana, mashed
- 1 egg
- 2 egg whites
- 1 cup maple syrup
- 1/3 cup of raw sugar, such as turbinado or demerara
- 1 tbsp vanilla extract
- 2 cups grated unpeeled zucchini
- 2 cups whole wheat pastry flour
- 1 tbsp ground cinnamon
- 1 cup unprocessed bran
- 1 tsp salt
- 1/4 tsp baking powder
- 1/2 tsp ground nutmeg
- 1/4 tsp ground cloves
- 1 tsp baking soda
- 1/4 tsp ground ginger
- 1/4 tsp ground allspice

Directions:

Heat the oven beforehand to 175°C or 350°F. Oil a baking pan that is 9x13 inches in size.

In a big bowl, mix egg whites, egg, banana, and pumpkin. Beat in vanilla, sugar, and maple syrup – this should become a little bubbly. Mix in zucchini and put it aside.

In a different bowl, mix allspice, ginger, cloves, nutmeg, cinnamon, baking powder, bran, baking soda, salt, and flour. In the zucchini mixture, put the flour mixture gradually while stirring to moisten all ingredients. The bather will be tough if it is over-mixed.

In the prepared pan, pour the batter. A toothpick put in the middle comes out clean after 50-60 minutes. Before slicing into squares, let it cool completely.

Recipe 16: Anytime Banana Bread

Brown yummy

Serving Size: 16

Cooking Time: 1 hour and 15 minutes

Ingredients:

- 1 1/2 cups all-purpose flour
- 1 tsp baking soda
- 1/2 tsp salt
- 1 cup white sugar
- 2 eggs, beaten
- 1/4 cup butter, melted
- 3 bananas, mashed

Directions:

Grease, then flour a 2 7x3-in. Loaf pans. Preheat your oven to 175°C/350°F.

Whisk sugar, salt, soda, and flour together in a bowl. Mix in mashed bananas, melted butter, and slightly beaten eggs. Mix nuts in if you want. Put into prepped pans.

Bake for an hour at 175°C/350°F until an inserted wooden toothpick in the middle exits cleanly.

Recipe 17: Oatmeal Bars

Tasty bars

Serving Size: 6

Cooking Time: 50 minutes

Ingredients:

- 3 cups old-fashioned oats
- 1 1/4 cups 2% milk
- 1/2 tsp ground cinnamon
- 1/2 cup white sugar
- 2 large eggs, beaten
- 1 tsp baking powder
- 1/2 tsp salt
- 1 over-ripe banana
- 1/2 cup unsweetened applesauce
- 2 tsp packed brown sugar

Directions:

In a bowl, mix white sugar and applesauce. Beat eggs, milk baking powder, salt, and oats to applesauce mix. Blend banana into oat mix. Place batter into baking dish.

In a small bowl, incorporate cinnamon and brown sugar. Place the mix on the banana batter.

Bake in the oven until it is firm for 30 to 35 minutes. For 5 minutes, cool.

Slice into bars.

Recipe 18: Bread Cookies

Delicious

Serving Size: 6

Cooking Time: 20 minutes

Ingredients:

- 4 tbsp Honey
- 3 1/2 tbsp melted coconut oil
- 2 beaten eggs
- 3/4 tsp vanilla extract
- 1/2 cup banana puree
- ¾ cup of oats (old-fashioned)
- 1 ¼ cups instant oats
- ¼ cup wheat germ (toasted)
- chopped walnuts(1/2 cup)
- 3/4 tsp cinnamon and 1/4 tsp nutmeg
- 1/3 cup Small-sized chocolate chips
- 1/4 tsp Salt

Directions:

Set aside a big baking sheet using parchment paper

Mix honey with molten coconut oil thoroughly in a bowl, then add the eggs inside

Whisk in both the vanilla extract and the puree, then instantly add in the oats, cinnamon, walnuts, wheat germ, salt, nutmeg, and mini-chocolate chips

Fold dry ingredients inside the wet ones until it's even.

After some time, Pre-heat the oven.

Heat for 18 minutes, then sprinkle some small chocolate chips on all the cookies.

Recipe 19: Banana Bread Brownies

If you love the taste of both brownies and banana bread, then this is one dish I know you won't be able to get enough of.

Serving Size: 24

Cooking Time: 35 minutes

Ingredients:

For the brownies:

- 2 eggs, beaten
- 3 bananas, mashed
- 1 ½ cups of white sugar
- 1 cup of sour cream
- ½ cup of butter, soft
- 2 tsp of pure vanilla
- 2 cups of white flour
- 1 tsp of baker's style baking soda
- ¾ tsp of salt
- ½ cup of walnuts, chopped

For the frosting:

- ½ cup of butter, soft
- 3 cups of powdered sugar
- 1 ½ tsp of pure vanilla
- 3 tbsp of whole milk

Directions:

Preheat the oven to 375 degrees. Grease a baking dish with cooking spray.

Prepare the brownie layer. Add in the white sugar, sour cream, soft butter, and beaten eggs in a bowl. Stir well to mix. Add in the mashed bananas and pure vanilla. Stir well until creamy in consistency.

Add in the baker's style baking soda, white flour, and a dash of salt. Stir well for 1 minute. Add in the chopped walnuts and fold gently to incorporate.

Pour into the baking dish. Place into the oven to bake for 25 minutes or until golden. Remove and set aside to cool.

Prepare the frosting. Melt the butter in a medium pot. Allow melting. Cook for 5 minutes or until browned. Add in the powdered sugar, pure vanilla, and whole milk. Whisk until smooth in consistency. Remove from heat.

Pour the frosting over the brownies. Cool for 15 minutes. Slice and serve.

Recipe 20: Banana Chocolate Pudding

Yummy pudding

Serving Size: 8

Cooking Time: 2 hours and 10 minutes

Ingredients:

- 1 Bread Loaf with the crust
- 1 quart Milk
- 3 Eggs
- 1 cup Sugar
- 2 tbsp Vanilla extract
- 4 ripe bananas, mashed
- 1 cup Raisins
- 1 tsp Fresh nutmeg
- 1 tsp Cinnamon
- Whipped cream: for serving

Directions:

Cut bread loaf to make small cubes, soak them in one bowl with milk, and leave for one hour.

Preheat an oven to almost 325°F. Grease a baking dish (9x13-inch).

Take a bowl and beat sugar, vanilla, and eggs together. Mix this blend in the bread mixture and toss spices, raisins, and mashed bananas in this bowl. Mix them well and pour this mixture into your greased baking dish.

Put in the middle of your oven to bake for almost 1 hour and ten minutes. Remove from your oven and leave at room temperature for 30 minutes. Serve with whipped cream.

Recipe 21: Banana Bread Cobbler

Cobbler is tasty

Serving Size: 8

Cooking Time: 50 minutes

Ingredients:

- 1 1/2 cups self-rising flour
- 1 cup granulated sugar
- 1 cup whole milk
- 1/2 cup unsalted butter, melted
- 4 ripe bananas, sliced
- 3/4 cup light brown sugar
- 1/2 cup unsalted butter, softened
- 1 cup quick-cooking oats
- 1/2 cup chopped pecans

Directions:

Preheat the oven to 375°. Spray an 11 x 7 baking dish with nonstick cooking spray. In a mixing bowl, add 1 cup self-rising flour, granulated sugar, and milk. Whisk until well combined and stir in 1/2 cup melted butter. Pour the batter into the baking dish.

Place the bananas over the batter. Add 1/2 cup self-rising flour, brown sugar, 1/2 cup softened butter, oats, and pecans in a small bowl. Gently mix the butter into the dry ingredients until coarse crumbs form. Toss the crumbs on the bananas

Bake for 40 minutes, or until the cobbler is bubbling and the topping is golden brown. Before serving, remove the cobbler from the heat and let it cool for 15 minutes. If preferred, top with vanilla ice cream or whipped cream.

Recipe 22: Banana Bread Cookies

Delicious chewy and soft cookies with the taste of home-cooked banana bread.

Serving Size: 36

Cooking Time: 1 hour

Ingredients:

- 1 tbsp milk
- 2 cups all-purpose flour
- 1 banana
- 1 cup butter flavored shortening
- 1 tsp vanilla extract
- 1 cup white sugar
- 1/2 tsp salt
- 2 eggs
- 3 tbsp butter
- 1/3 cup confectioners' sugar
- 1 tsp baking soda

Directions:

Set an oven to 175°C (350°F) and start preheating. Coat the baking sheets lightly with cooking spray.

Cream white sugar and shortening together in a medium bowl until they become smooth. Whisk in banana, vanilla extract, and eggs. Mix salt, baking soda, and flour; add into the shortening mixture and combine thoroughly to have a sticky batter. Add onto the greased baking sheets by rounded tbsp

In the prepared oven, bake until browned lightly, or for 10-15 minutes.

Combine the vanilla extract, milk, confectioners' sugar, and butter in a medium bowl. Change the amount of milk as needed to reach the drizzling consistency. Sprinkle on top of the warm cookies.

Recipe 23: Donuts with Browned Butter Caramel Glaze

Yummy donuts

Serving Size: 6

Cooking Time: 20 minutes

Ingredients:

Doughnuts

- 1 big egg
- 1/2 cup Packed brown sugar
- 1/4 cup Ground sugar
- 1/4 cup Vegetable oil or canola
- 1/4 cup Sour cream
- 2 tsp vanilla concentrate
- 1 cup Crushed ripe bananas.
- 1 ¼ cups of Flour (all-purpose)
- 1/2 tsp Baking powder & baking soda
- Salt (to taste)
- 1/4 cup of unsalted spread, sautéed
- 1/3 cup light brown colored stuffed sugar
- 3 tbsp cream (1/2-and-1/2)
- 2 cups confectioners' filtered sugar
- 1/2 tsp vanilla concentrate

Directions:

Doughnuts – Preheat your broiler.

Shower one six-count doughnut container.

Include sugars, oil, egg, vanilla, sour cream.

Add bananas and mix.

Toss in the salt, baking soda, flour, and baking powder.

Turn-out batter into an arranged container, filling every cavity to 2/3 to ¾.

Bake for around fourteen minutes.

Recipe 24: Banana Bread French Toast

A decadent breakfast treat.

Serving Size: 4

Cooking Time: 15 minutes

64

Ingredients:

- 3 eggs
- 3 tbsp sweetened condensed milk
- 1 tsp vanilla extract
- 2 tbsp butter
- 1 loaf banana bread
- confectioners' sugar for dusting (optional)

Directions:

Use a fork to Mix the vanilla, condensed milk, and eggs in a shallow bowl; put aside.

Oil and heat butter in a pan. Cut banana bread and put in the egg mixture, dip each slice; put it in the hot pan. Cook each side till golden brown; if desired, dust with confectioners' sugar. Serve.

Recipe 25: Banana Bread from Motts

Give an old favorite a new spin. It's a healthier choice thanks to the applesauce, which adds flavor without losing nutrition.

Serving Size: 16

Cooking Time: 55 minutes

Ingredients:

- 2 tbsp vegetable oil
- 1/2 cup Mott's® Natural Applesauce
- 1/2 tsp ground allspice
- 2 1/2 cups all-purpose flour
- 4 medium ripe bananas, mashed
- 1 cup sugar
- 2 tsp baking soda
- 3 egg whites
- 2 tsp baking powder
- 1 tsp vanilla extract

Directions:

Preheat the oven to 375 degrees Fahrenheit. Nonstick cooking spray an 8 1/2 x 4 1/2-inch loaf pan. Combine baking powder, flour, baking soda, and allspice in a large mixing basin.

Combine applesauce, vanilla, egg whites, sugar, bananas, and oil in a medium mixing dish.

A toothpick inserted in the cake's center should come out clean after 60 minutes. Cool in the pan for 10 minutes. Invert the pan onto a wire rack. Lie the right side up. Allow cooling fully.

Recipe 26: Banana Bread Muffins

Tasty muffins

Serving Size: 16

Cooking Time: 35 minutes

Ingredients:

- 2 cups Flour
- 1 tsp Baking soda
- 1/4 tsp Salt
- 1/2 cup Stick butter
- 3/4 cup Brown sugar
- 2 Beaten eggs, large
- 3 to 4 over ripe bananas

Directions:

Preheat your oven to almost 350°F. Line your muffin tins with baking papers and spray with cooking spray.

Take one bowl and combine salt, soda, and flour in this bowl.

Take another bowl to combine sugar and butter. Whisk them together and stir in mashed bananas and eggs. Mix them well to make a smooth blend. Add this mixture to your flour mixture and whisk them well to get a consistent batter. You can use an electric mixer.

Fill your muffin tins with banana batter and bake for almost 20 minutes. Check with a toothpick; if it is clean, the muffins are ready. If the toothpick is soiled, you can bake muffins for 5 minutes again.

Recipe 27: Banana Cream Cheese Glaze

Creamy cheese

Serving Size: 6

Cooking Time: 20 minutes

Ingredients:

Pancakes

- A couple of all-purpose flour
- 1 tsp baking powder
- 1/2 tsp baking soda
- 1/2 tsp salt
- 1/2 tsp ground cinnamon
- 3/4 cup buttermilk
- 1/4 cup acrid cream
- 3 tbsp ground sugar
- 3 tbsp brown sugar
- 1 1/2 cups squashed overripe bananas
- 1 big egg
- 1/2 tsp vanilla concentrate
- 4 tbsp dissolved unsalted butter
- 1 1/2 cups powdered sugar

Directions:

Preheat an electric frying pan and whisk the baking soda, cinnamon, flour, salt, and baking powder for 20 seconds.

Whisk dissolved butter, vanilla, egg, mashed bananas, brown sugar, ground sugar, sour cream, and buttermilk in a different bowl.

Empty buttermilk blend into the flour mix.

Cook till base is brilliant brown and do the same for the other side.

Recipe 28: Bread Protein Waffles

Protein waffles

Serving Size: 4

Cooking Time: 10 minutes

Ingredients:

- 1 cup oat flour
- 1/2 cup vanilla protein powder
- 1/2 cup coconut flour
- 1/2 tsp ground cinnamon
- 1/4 tsp salt
- 1 cup of almond milk
- 1 tsp vanilla concentrate

Directions:

Preheat

Mix all the salt, oat flour, cinnamon, coconut flour, and protein powder. Blend until simply consolidated.

Blend the banana, vanilla, and milk.

Serve right away.

Recipe 29: Banana Bread Pudding

Creamy pudding

Serving Size: 6

Cooking Time: 1 hour

Ingredients:

- 4 cups day-old sourdough bread, cubed
- 1/4 cup unsalted butter, melted
- 3 eggs
- 2 3/4 cups whole milk
- 1/2 cup plus 2 tbs. granulated sugar
- 3 tsp vanilla extract
- 1/2 tsp ground cinnamon
- 1/2 tsp ground nutmeg
- 1/2 tsp salt
- 1 cup sliced banana
- 3 tbsp unsalted butter
- 1 tbsp cornstarch
- 1/4 cup light corn syrup

Directions:

Using nonstick cooking spray, coat a 2-quart casserole dish. Preheat the oven to 375 degrees Fahrenheit. In a casserole dish, place the bread cubes. 1/4 cup melted butter should be poured over the bread pieces. Toss the bread pieces in the butter until they are completely covered.

Add the eggs, 2 cups milk, 1/2 cup granulated sugar, 2 tsp vanilla extract, cinnamon, nutmeg, and salt in a mixing bowl. Pour over the bread chunks. Add the bananas to the dish and stir until all the ingredients are coated in the liquid.

A knife stabbed in the center of the pudding should come out clean after 40 minutes. Cool the pudding while you make the sauce.

Combine 3 tbsp butter, cornstarch, 2 tsp granulated sugar, 3/4 cup milk, and corn syrup in a sauce pan over medium heat. Cook, stirring continuously until the sauce reaches a full boil. Boil the sauce for 1 minute and remove the pan from the heat. Stir in 1 tsp vanilla extract. Serve the sauce over servings of the bread pudding.

Recipe 30: Banana Streusel Muffins

Well-done muffins

Serving Size: 12

Cooking Time: 35 minutes

Ingredients:

- 2 cups All-purpose flour
- 1 tsp baking soda
- 1 cup of sugar
- 1/2 tsp salt
- 1/2 tsp baking powder
- 1/4 tsp cinnamon ground
- 2 eggs
- 1 cup sour cream eight ounces
- 1/4 cup molten butter
- 2 medium-level ripe bananas (squashed)
- 1/2 cup minced walnuts

Cinnamon streusel:

- 1/2 cup of brown sugar
- 3 tbsp flour (all-purpose)
- 1/4 tsp cinnamon ground
- 4 tbsp relaxed bread

Directions:

Preheat stove and arranged a muffin container.

Empty the flour, cinnamon, baking soda, salt, baking powder, and sugar.

Mix with eggs, bananas, butter, and sour cream, spread, and bananas.

Recipe 31: Banana Chia Seeds

Yummy

Serving Size: 15

Cooking Time: 15 minutes

Ingredients:

- 1 ½ cups of white sugar
- ½ cup of butter softened
- 3 bananas, mashed
- 2 eggs
- 2 cups of all-purpose flour
- ½ tsp of baking soda
- 1/3 cup of sour milk
- ¼ tsp of salt
- 1 tsp of vanilla extract
- ½ cup of chia seeds

Directions:

Preheat oven to 350 degrees F and lightly grease an 8x4-inch loaf pan.

Mix eggs, flour, chia seeds , baking soda, vanilla extract, butter, sour milk, salt, bananas, and sugar in a large mixing bowl. Beat until well blended.

Pour batter into loaf pan.

A toothpick inserted into the bread should be clean.

Let cool for 10 minutes before serving.

Recipe 32: Banana Bread with Chocolate Filling

Presentable chocolate filling

Serving Size: 8

Cooking Time: 1 hour and 20 minutes

Ingredients:

- Melted butter: 1/2 cup and some extra to grease pan
- All-purpose flour: 1 cup + 2 Tbsp
- Baking soda: 1 tsp
- Kosher salt: 1/4 tsp
- Sugar: 3/4 cup + 2 tbsp
- Buttermilk: 1/4 cup
- Vanilla extract: 1 tsp
- 2 eggs + 1 Egg yolk
- Ripe bananas (mashed): 3
- Melted chocolate: 1 cup

Directions:

Preheat an oven to almost 350° F. Grease one loaf pan with butter and sprinkle some flour (9x5-inch).

Take one bowl and whisk baking soda, salt, and flour (1 cup) together.

Take another bowl and combine one egg yolk, one egg, vanilla, buttermilk, butter, and sugar (3/4 cup) in this bowl. To combine the wet and dry components, pour the wet ingredients over the dry ones and stir thoroughly. Toss in mashed bananas.

Chocolate Filling:

Take one bowl and mix melted chocolate, remaining sugar, flour, and egg in this bowl.

Transfer 1/2 batter into greased pan and dollop cheese filling on the top. Make a smooth layer with a spatula and top with leftover dough.

Bake in your preheated oven for almost 50 - 60 minutes and use a cake tester or toothpick to check the cake's doneness. If the bread is ready, keep it in its pan for almost ten minutes and put it on your wire rack. Serve.

Recipe 33: Banana Bread with Cream Cheese

Appetizing cheese

Serving Size: 16

Cooking Time: 15 minutes

Ingredients:

- ½ cup of margarine
- ½ tsp of baking soda
- 1 8-ounce package of cream cheese
- 1 ½ tsp of baking powder
- 1 ¼ cups of white sugar
- 2 eggs
- 1 cup of mashed bananas
- 2 ¼ cups of all-purpose flour
- ¾ cup of chopped pecans
- 2 tbsp of brown sugar
- 1 tsp of vanilla extract
- 2 tsp of ground cinnamon

Directions:

In a large bowl, cream together margarine and cream cheese. Add the white sugar and beat until fluffy. Gradually add the eggs and make sure to beat well after each addition. Stir in bananas and vanilla.

Combine all-purpose flour, baking soda, and salt in a separate basin. Stir the flour mixture into the margarine mixture until it is barely moistened.

Mix nuts, cinnamon, and brown sugar. Remove from the oven and let cool for 10 minutes.

Recipe 34: Banana Bread with Maple Flavor

It is time to enjoy maple flavor with your favorite banana bread. The recipe is really easy.

Serving Size: 12

Cooking Time: 1 hour and 20 minutes

Ingredients:

- Melted butter: 1/2 cup
- Maple syrup: 1/2 cup
- Egg: 1
- Bananas: 2 ripe
- Maple extract: 1/2 tsp
- Milk: 3 tbsp
- Chopped walnuts: 1/4 cup
- All-purpose flour: 2 cups
- Baking soda: 1 tsp
- Baking powder: 1/2 tsp
- White sugar: 3 tbsp

Directions:

Preheat your oven to almost 350 °F. Grease one loaf pan (5x9-inch).

Take one bowl and mix maple syrup and melted butter. Whisk in bananas and eggs, leave a few banana chunks. Mix in milk and maple extract.

Take one separate bowl and mix baking powder, baking soda, and flour in this bowl. Add to the banana mixture to moisten all ingredients. Place in a greased loaf pan. Sprinkle sugar and nuts evenly over batter.

Bake in your preheated oven for almost 50 minutes to make it golden brown. Check with a knife by inserting it in the middle of the loaf.

Recipe 35: Banana Bread with Mayonnaise

Tasty bread

Serving Size: 12

Cooking Time: 10 minutes

Ingredients:

- 1 ½ cups of all-purpose flour
- 1 cup of white sugar
- 1 tsp of baking soda
- 1 tsp of salt
- 1 egg
- ½ cup of light mayonnaise
- 1 tsp of vanilla extract
- 3 ripe bananas, mashed

Directions:

In a large bowl, beat the egg and stir in mayonnaise, bananas, and vanilla. Stir until well blended.

Combine flour, sugar, baking soda, and salt. Stir in the banana mixture until smooth.

Pour batter into loaf pan.

The toothpick test should come out clean after 45 minutes in the oven.

Let cool for 10 minutes before serving.

Recipe 36: Banana Bread with Oat-Streusel Topping

Oat topping

Serving Size: 16

Cooking Time: 2 hours and 5 minutes

Ingredients:

- 1/4 cup of cold butter, cut into small pieces
- 1/2 cup all-purpose flour
- 1 1/4 cups white sugar
- 1/4 cup packed brown sugar
- 1 tsp ground cinnamon
- 1/2 cup quick-cooking oats
- 1/2 cup butter, softened
- 2 eggs
- 3 ripe bananas, mashed
- 1/2 cup buttermilk
- 1 tsp vanilla extract
- 2 1/2 cups all-purpose flour
- 2 tsp pumpkin pie spice
- 2 tsp baking powder
- 1/2 tsp ground cinnamon
- 1 cup chopped nuts (optional)

Directions:

Preheat oven to 175°C/350°F, then greases 2 8 1/2 x 4 1/2-in. Loaf pans.

Streusel topping: Mix oats, 1 tsp Cinnamon, brown sugar, 1/2 cup flour, and 1/2 cup cut-up butter till crumbly in a bowl; put aside.

Cream butter and sugar in a bowl; mix eggs in. Add vanilla extract, buttermilk, and bananas; mix till mixture is blended well. Beat nuts, cinnamon, baking powder, pumpkin pie spice, and flour in.

Put batter in prepped loaf pan; sprinkle 1/2 streusel topping over each loaf.

In the preheated oven, bake for 1 hour 15 minutes till topping is browned and loaves rise; cool banana bread for 5 minutes in pans. Turn out on wire rack; finish cooling.

Recipe 37: Banana Bread with Salted Caramel

Caramel meal

Serving Size: 12

Cooking Time: 1 hour and 20 minutes

Ingredients:

- Melted butter: 1/2 cup + little more to grease pain
- All-purpose flour: 1 cup + little more to dust pan
- Baking soda: 1 tsp
- Kosher salt: 1/4 tsp
- Sugar: 3/4 cup
- Buttermilk: 1/4 cup
- Vanilla extract: 1 tsp
- Egg: 1 large + Egg yolk
- Ripe bananas: 4 (3 mashed + make slices with one leftover banana)
- Caramel: 1/2 cup + little more for drizzling

Directions:

Preheat an oven to almost 350° F. Grease and dust one loaf pan (9x5-inch).

Take one large bowl and combine salt, baking soda, and flour in this bowl. Take one separate bowl and cream sugar, egg yolk, egg, vanilla, buttermilk, and butter together. Mix in mashed bananas to make a smooth blend. Stir flour mixture and caramel into the banana mixture and stir well to moist everything. Pour batter into your greased pan. Scatter banana slices over batter.

Bake in your preheated oven for almost 65 minutes. Check with a toothpick or cake tester. Wait for 10 minutes and transfer bread on your cooling rack. Drizzle with some caramel and serve.

Recipe 38: Banana Bread with Vanilla Pudding

Vanilla pudding

Serving Size: 12

Cooking Time: 15 minutes

Ingredients:

- 1 ¾ cups of all-purpose flour
- 1 ¼ tsp of baking powder
- ½ tsp of baking soda
- ¾ tsp of salt
- 1 3-ounce package of non-instant vanilla pudding mix
- 2/3 cup of white sugar
- ½ cup of shortening
- 2 eggs
- 2 tbsp of milk
- 1 1/3 cups of mashed bananas
- 1/3 cup of chopped walnuts

Directions:

Preheat oven to 350F and gently oil an 8x4-inch loaf pan.

Cream shortening and sugar together in a large mixing basin. Add the eggs, mashed bananas, and milk and beat.

Mix flour, baking soda, baking powder, vanilla pudding, and salt in a separate bowl. Add to the banana mixture.

Stir in nuts to the batter.

Pour batter into loaf pan.

Preheat oven to 350°F.

Remove the pan from the oven and set it aside for 10 minutes to cool.

Recipe 39: Banana Bread with Walnuts

Walnuts meal

Serving Size: 15

Cooking Time: 20 minutes

Ingredients:

- ½ cup of butter, melted
- 1 ½ cups of all-purpose flour
- 2 medium bananas
- 2 eggs, beaten
- 1 tsp of baking soda
- 1 tsp of vanilla extract
- ½ tsp of salt
- 1 cup of white sugar
- ½ cup of sour cream
- ½ cup of chopped walnuts

Directions:

Combine baking soda, all-purpose flour, and salt in a large mixing basin. Butter and sugar should be combined in a separate big mixing dish. In a separate bowl, whisk together the beaten eggs and vanilla extract. Pour the butter mixture into the flour mixture and whisk until everything is well combined. Stir in the sour cream, walnuts, and bananas until thoroughly combined.

Spoon the batter into the loaf pan.

Remove from the oven and set aside to cool for 10 minutes before serving.

Recipe 40: Banana Butterscotch Bread

This variation of banana bread is addicting.

Serving Size: 24

Cooking Time: 2 hours and 40 minutes

Ingredients:

- 2 cups all-purpose flour
- 1 tsp baking powder
- 1/2 tsp baking soda
- 1/2 tsp salt
- 3/4 tsp ground cinnamon
- 1/2 tsp ground nutmeg
- 1/2 cup butter
- 3/4 cup white sugar
- 1 large egg
- 3 ripe bananas, mashed
- 3/4 cup butterscotch chips
- 1/2 cup chopped walnuts (optional)

Directions:

Preheat the oven to 175 °C or 350 °F. Lightly oil 2 loaf pans, 9x5-inch in size. Put aside. Sift together the baking soda, nutmeg, flour, salt, cinnamon, and baking powder in a bowl. Put aside.

Using an electric mixer, whip sugar and butter in a big bowl till fluffy and light. The mixture should be paler in color. Whip in egg, then mix in mashed bananas. Add in flour mixture, stirring till just blended. Fold in walnuts and butterscotch chips, stirring just enough to blend evenly. Into the prepped pans, evenly transfer the batter.

Bake for 25 to 28 minutes in the prepped oven until an inserted toothpick into the middle gets out clean. Let it cool for 10 minutes in pans before transferring on a wire rack to fully cool.

Recipe 41: Banana Chai Bread

Low-fat banana bread recipe with chai flavor!

Serving Size: 12

Cooking Time: 55 minutes

Ingredients:

- 1 tbsp baking powder
- 1 3/4 cups all-purpose flour
- 1/2 tsp salt
- 3/4 cup white sugar
- 1/2 cup low fat cream cheese
- 2 eggs
- 3/4 cup mashed bananas
- 1/4 cup brewed chai tea

Directions:

Mix salt, baking powder, and flour in a medium bowl.

Mix eggs, cream cheese, and sugar till fluffy and light in another bowl; mix Chai and mashed bananas into cream cheese mixture, then add flour mixture. Stir till smooth.

Put the mixture in 9x5-in. Greased loaf pan.

In preheated 175°C/350°F oven, bake for 1 hour; cool on a rack. After 10 minutes, remove from pan.

Recipe 42: Banana Chip Bread

I love making this for my relatives.

Serving Size: 4

Cooking Time: 1 hour and 15 minutes

Ingredients:

- 1/2 cup butter, softened
- 1 cup sugar
- 1 egg
- 1 cup of mashed ripe bananas
- 3 tbsp milk
- 2 cups all-purpose flour
- 1 tsp baking powder
- 1/2 tsp baking soda
- 1 cup (6-ounce) semisweet chocolate chips
- 1/2 cup chopped pecans

Directions:

In a large mixing bowl, beat the sugar and butter until creamy. Mix milk and bananas in a small bowl. Mix baking soda, baking powder, and flour; alternately with banana mixture, add to creamed mixture. Fold pecans and chocolate chips in.

Put in 9x5-in. Greased loaf pan; bake for 60-70 minutes at 350° till an inserted toothpick in the middle exits cleanly before transferring from pan onto a wire rack to completely cool, cool for 10 minutes.

Recipe 43: Banana-Chip Nut Bread

Enjoy this delightful bread, chocolate chips, and walnuts are a nice complement to mild banana flavor.

Serving Size: 6

Cooking Time: 50 minutes

Ingredients:

- 1 tbsp Plus 1-1/2 tsp butter softened
- 1 tbsp Plus 1-1/2 tsp brown sugar
- 2 tbsp beaten egg
- 1 medium ripe banana
- 1-1/2 tsp buttermilk
- 1/3 cup white rice flour
- 1/3 cup tapioca flour
- 1-1/2 tsp mashed potato flakes
- 3/4 tsp baking powder
- 1/8 tsp baking soda
- 1/8 tsp salt
- 2 tbsp chopped walnuts
- 2 tbsp semisweet chocolate chips

Directions:

In a small mixing bowl, cream together brown sugar and butter. Put in egg; combine well. Crush banana with buttermilk in a small bowl. Put together the salt, baking soda, baking powder, potato flakes, and flours; put into creamed mixture alternately with the banana mixture till just moistened. Fold in chocolate chips and walnuts.

Put into a loaf pan of 5-3/4x3x2-inch in size coated with cooking spray. Allow baking at 350° for 30 to 35 minutes till a toothpick pricked in the middle comes out clean. Allow cooling for 10 minutes on a wire rack.

Recipe 44: Banana Chocolate Chip Bread

A moist and yummy banana bread recipe.

Serving Size: 10

Cooking Time: 1 hour and 25 minutes

Ingredients:

- 1 tsp salt
- 1 tsp baking powder
- 3 ripe bananas
- 1 tbsp milk
- 1 tsp baking soda
- 1 tsp the ground cinnamon, or to taste
- 1/2 cup butter, softened
- 1 cup white sugar
- 2 cups all-purpose flour
- 2 eggs
- 1 cup semisweet chocolate chips

Directions:

In a mixing basin, combine the salt, baking soda, baking powder, and flour. In a separate dish, combine the cinnamon, milk, and bananas. In a third bowl, cream together the sugar and butter until frothy and light. Mix the eggs and banana mixture into butter mixture. Mix the dry mixture in till blended. Fold chocolate chips in just till combined. Put batter in a prepped loaf pan.

In a preheated oven, bake for 70 minutes till an inserted toothpick in the middle exits clean. Transfer to a wire rack to cool fully before slicing after 10 minutes.

Recipe 45: Banana Chocolate Chip Muffins

Chocolate chips

Serving Size: 5

Cooking Time: 20 minutes

Ingredients:

- 2 cups all-purpose flour
- 1/3 cup white sugar
- 2 tbsp Dutch-process cocoa powder
- 1 tbsp baking powder
- 1 cup mashed bananas
- 2/3 cup canola oil
- 1 egg, beaten
- 1 cup semi-sweet chocolate chips

Directions:

Stir in the flour and sugar until well combined.

Combine the egg, bananas, and oil in a separate bowl. Mix it into the dry mixture until well combined. Add in the chocolate chips, then fold. Fill a greased muffin tray 3/4 full with the batter.

Put in the preheated 425°F (220°C) oven and bake for 15-20 minutes. Take out the muffins and let them fully cool down on a wire rack.

Recipe 46: Banana Flaxseed Muffins

Healthy and gluten-free muffins!

Serving Size: 12

Cooking Time: 45 minutes

Ingredients:

- 1 1/2 tsp butter
- 3 ripe mashed bananas
- 1/4 cup white sugar
- 1 1/4 cups flaxseed meal
- 1 tbsp baking powder
- 3 eggs, beaten
- 1 apple
- 2 tbsp chia seeds
- 1/2 cup of coconut flakes, or more to taste
- 1 1/2 tsp ground cinnamon

Directions:

Set oven to preheat at 350°F (175°C). Use butter to grease a muffin tin.

Mix sugar, flaxseed meal, baking powder, chia seeds, and cinnamon in a bowl. Add eggs, apples, and bananas. Mix well. Add 6 tbsp Of coconut flakes, mix. Pour the batter until the muffin tin is 3/4 full. Top with the remaining 2 tbsp of coconut flakes.

Bake for 1/2 an hour until the top springs back when lightly touched.

Recipe 47: Banana Coconut Loaf

A pretty loaf recipe that's so yummy.

Serving Size: 12

Cooking Time: 1 hour and 25 minutes

Ingredients:

- 2 eggs
- 1/2 cup butter
- 1 cup mashed bananas
- 1/2 tsp almond extract
- 1 1/2 tsp baking powder
- 1/2 cup flaked coconut
- 1/2 tsp baking soda
- 1/2 tsp salt
- 1 1/2 cups all-purpose flour
- 1/2 cup chopped walnuts
- 1/2 cup maraschino cherries
- 1 cup white sugar

Directions:

Mix cherries, chopped walnuts, salt, baking soda, baking powder, coconut, and flour.

Break eggs into mixing bowl; beat till frothy and light. Add melted butter/margarine and sugar; beat well. Mix flavoring and mashed banana in. Add flour mixture; mix to combine. Put in 9x5x3-in. Greased loaf pan.

Bake for 1 hour at 175°C/350°F till an inserted toothpick in the middle exits clean. Stand for 10 minutes; remove from pan, then cool.

Recipe 48: Banana Cranberry Bread

I always have leftover cranberry sauce after Thanksgiving, so I created this very moist and delicious recipe.

Serving Size: 24

Cooking Time: 1 hour and 30 minutes

Ingredients:

- 2 1/2 cups white sugar
- 1 1/2 tsp baking powder
- 1 cup shortening
- 3 eggs
- 3 mashed bananas
- 1 1/2 tsp baking soda
- 1 cup cranberry sauce
- 1/2 tsp ground nutmeg
- 1/2 cup milk
- 1 tsp vanilla extract
- 4 cups all-purpose flour
- 1 tsp ground cinnamon
- 1/2 cup chopped walnuts

Directions:

Preheat oven to 350°F (175 degrees C). Grease two 9x5 loaf pans.

In a large mixing bowl, beat together the sugar and shortening until light and fluffy. Stir in bananas, cranberry sauce, milk, flour, baking soda, baking powder, cinnamon, vanilla, and nutmeg. Blend in the flour mixture gradually. Add walnuts. Pour into loaf pans.

The toothpick test should come out clean after 50-60 minutes in the preheated oven. Then put out onto a wire rack and cool fully.

Recipe 49: Banana Date Flaxseed Bread

Healthy bread with the nutty flavor of flaxseeds.

Serving Size: 10

Cooking Time: 1 hour and 5 minutes

Ingredients:

- 1/2 tsp baking soda
- 1/2 cup flax seed
- 1 1/2 cups all-purpose flour
- 3 bananas, mashed
- 1/4 cup vegetable oil
- 1/2 tsp baking powder
- 1/2 tsp salt
- 1/4 cup flax seed
- 2 eggs
- 1/2 cup chopped pitted dates
- 1/2 cup white sugar

Directions:

Preheat the oven to 175°C or 350°F. Grease an 8-inch by 4-inch loaf pan lightly. Grind a 1/2 cup of flax seeds in a food processor or electric coffee grinder; set aside.

Whisk eggs, banana, sugar, and oil together in a big mixing bowl. Combine a quarter cup whole flax seed, flour, ground flax seed, baking powder, salt, and baking soda in another bowl; mix with the banana mixture. Stir in dates. Ladle batter in the greased loaf pan.

Bake for 55-60 mins in the preheated oven until an inserted skewer in the middle of the loaf comes out without residue.

Recipe 50: Banana Eggnog Bread

This warm banana bread with a glass of eggnog is my favorite snack. I combined the two, and the results came out perfect!

Serving Size: 16

Cooking Time: 1 hour and 10 minutes

Ingredients:

- 1 tsp vanilla extract
- 1 tsp baking powder
- 1-1/2 cups sugar
- 2 large eggs
- 1/8 tsp baking soda
- 1 cup of mashed ripe bananas
- 1/4 cup eggnog
- 1/2 cup butter
- 1-3/4 cups all-purpose flour
- 1/4 tsp salt
- 1/2 tsp ground nutmeg

Directions:

Heat oven to 350 degrees beforehand. Cream the sugar and butter together in a large mixing basin until light and creamy. Put eggs in one by one, mixing well after each. Whip in vanilla, eggnog, and bananas. Mix baking soda, salt, 1/4 tsp Nutmeg, baking powder, and flour in another bowl; mix into banana mixture slowly.

Pour into a greased 9x5-in. Loaf pan; garnish with remaining nutmeg. Bake for 50-60 minutes. Rest 10 minutes in the pan before taking it out to a wire rack to cool.

Conclusion

Banana bread, as the name suggests, is made up of bananas (duh) and, while the ingredients differ slightly depending on what style of a loaf is being made, it is primarily white or wholemeal flour, ripe bananas, a fat (e.g., butter, margarine, cooking oil, milk chocolate or fruit jam), eggs and a liquid to bind it all together (e.g., milk, juice, water or a non-dairy alternative for vegans). Banana also happens to be the most common type of fruit consumed in the entire world, whittled down to nothing more than a sour pulp which is then heated and mashed up – irrefutably, it is a mass of recipes that fall in this category.

Unlike many other fruit bread, banana bread is very easy to serve and is often divided into firm slices and served with butter and jam, and/or cheese. It is also spectacularly quick to make since there are no complicated techniques, and there is no need to wait for the dough to prove. It can be baked simply and quickly and is generally low in fat and pretty healthy. Bake a loaf, and you'll be glad of it afterward, if only because a cup of tea goes down just as well with a slice as it does a biscuit.

The bread comes in different variations. Some bread has nuts in them, and others may have raisins, chocolate chips, cinnamon, blueberries, or raspberries.

You did encounter different variations of banana bread recipes in this book! So, what are you waiting for? These 300 recipes are so amazing that one cannot resist trying making them! Try them making them now!

Afterthoughts

I've been writing recipe books for some time now, and do you know what's the best feeling about it? Well, it's the chance to put my ideas down so that everyone can try them out, and not just me. It's always more fun when others have a chance to enjoy the recipes I enjoy.

However, I still try to make things simpler so that everyone can have a go at them. No matter the experience levels. In fact, I had feedbacks from top chefs and people who never stopped inside a kitchen. They loved the simplicity of the recipes and yet how delicious they have turned out.

That's why please do leave honest feedback. It will help everyone in deciding which book they need and it will help me become even better at my work. Also, share your favorite recipes from this book and maybe I'll create a book collection of my reader's favorite recipes.

Thanks

Brian White

About the Author

Sometimes it takes time to find out your career path. Going through a few changes in lifestyle, job positions and even forgetting about your college. Well, Brian White didn't know anything about cooking, recipes, and not even recipe writing, well not until he discovered one cookbook of his great, great mother.

Then he decided not to proceed with a career according to his college major and try his luck in cooking. The first couple of years were the most difficult ones. He had to take classes even for the cooking basics. But as he started to go deeper into the field it because of the love of his life.

Now, his goal is to help everyone, well, those who want to learn how to cook and those who want to learn more recipes and prepare dishes for the whole family.

In fact, he didn't want to limit himself to only one type of cooking so he started writing books on many different topics. Because in his point of you this was the only way he can reach more people.

Now, men and women are constantly in touch with him, asking for help and even requesting unique recipes for special occasions. His experience led to cookbooks that bring joy to the one making the dish and to those who are eating it.

Even today, he is not stopping. Brian White continues to create cookbooks and he won't stop, well not for a long, long time. So, you should definitely expect more cookbooks of his own creating every now and then.

Printed in Great Britain
by Amazon